blessed beyond Measure!

Sharr

Even Boss Ladies Need a Break!

45 Lessons in Intentionally Loving YOU

Written by Shar'ron Mason, MA, LMFT

Even Boss Ladies Need a Break!
Copyright © 2019 by Shar'ron Mason

ISBN (978-0-578-46870-9)

Dedication

I continue to be blown away by God's faithfulness towards me. He desires for my soul to sing in praises to Him and He provides me with the peace and joy to make that possible. To Him, the King of kings and Lord of lords I am grateful!

I dedicate this book to my cheerleaders: my Honey (Darrell), my Mama, my Daddy, my brothers, Brian, Joseph and Nickolas (RIH), to my family and my friends who continue to support me throughout my journey. Thank you for your prayers, your words of wisdom and for all that you do on my behalf. I love and appreciate each of you for your special place in my life, in my heart.

Special shout out to my daughter, Breonna, for doing all of the above and for my awesome cover pic. You are an amazing daughter!

I'd also like to thank my accountability partners/girl friends, La Tonya and Tiana, for your encouragement, support and continuing to fire me up.

Thanks to my editor, Ashley, for once again taking good care of my work.

Table of Contents

Introduction

Introduction

Whether you're climbing the corporate ladder, homeschooling your littles or making major moves in your own business, you know all too well the many demands and expectations placed on you as a woman. Many of these expectations have been passed on to you like a baton. Heck, some of these you've placed on yourself. Regardless of how you got to the place of being placed on the back burner, out of balance and overwhelmed, this book is for you BOSS LADY. I, too, wear many hats...wife, mother, grandmother, therapist, coach, author, speaker...oh, and last, but most important, child of God. I know full well that even the BOSS LADY needs a break!

Be a best friend to yourself today. Speak encouragement, offer forgiveness, comfort… Seek what makes your soul sing!

What's a best friend? Does she call you on your mess? Does he pick you up when you're down? Is she a great listener? Is he down for a good time, day or night? I've heard best friends refer to one another as soul mates. I've heard married individuals say their mates are their best friends. There is absolutely nothing wrong with having a best friend, matter of fact, having someone who is there for you through good and bad times make all moments richer and the worst moments tolerable. What would it look like if you were a best friend to yourself? Would you check in with yourself to make sure that you were ok? Would you comfort yourself when things weren't going as planned? Would you offer forgiveness for wrong choices made and seek to keep the relationship strong? Would you strive to get to know yourself better so that you could be the best friend possible? Always available, always in tune, and always willing to meet your needs. This may not be your experience of a best friend or may not even be realistic, but you can be all that and more to yourself.

We can run and hide from the world, but we can't hide from self. What changes do you need to make to create the YOU that you can't wait to come home to?

There's a face that I show on social media. There's a face that my husband sees. My goal is for both faces to be as authentically me as possible, but in reality he gets more "me" than my followers could ever get. And even as close as he and I are, there are still parts of me that can be concealed (to an extent). I can hide from the world, but I can't hide from myself. *You* can hide from the world, but you can't hide from yourself. From insecurities, to fears, to all the little quirky parts, they're all there. So, what do you want to do with it? What does the you that *you'd* want to come home to look like? Do you have a picture in your mind? Create that girl! She may be more confident or bold. She may be a little kinder or a lot less irritable. She may be more appreciative or less of a push over. She may be an all around happier person with more zest for life, or willing to try love again. Don't settle for anything less than what you truly want for yourself. Create the YOU that you can't wait to come home to!

Work, responsibilities and obligations all have their place, but where does play and fun come in? Don't wait until the weekend, seize the moment for a little fun today!

I once heard it said that if you're going to die at 29, 30 is old and if you're going to live until you're 90, 60 is young. That is oh so true, but in reality, most people don't know when they're going to pass from this earthly realm. Some would argue that that's the reason why they go so hard, so that they can leave a legacy to those they leave behind. I believe that it's important to enjoy each day of life to the fullest. That doesn't mean that you fall into neglect mode, but it does mean that you leave space for a little (or lot) of fun along the way. Does each day consist of getting up, getting out, working hard, going in and laying down, only to do it all again the next day? Waah, waah, waah, waah, waah, waah, waah! That's all I'm saying. Burn out is a real thing. It doesn't have to be that way. Do you feel that you have to earn a good time or fun? Do you believe that you just haven't done enough yet? You're an adult and you don't have to ask permission to enjoy this one life you have to live, whether you're 29 or 89. Enjoy your life, TODAY!

From what brings happiness, to what constitutes success, life has a way of selling us lies. Dispel the lies to create the purposeful life you want to live.

Lies! Lies! Lies! If you're not careful you'll be loaded down with baggage of lies and not even know that you're toting them around, let alone who sold them to you. Let's look at happiness. Were you told that a mate, some babies, a nice house and an account full of money would get you the golden ticket of happiness? If so, you probably strived for them only to realize that they didn't bring lasting happiness. Happiness comes through connecting with the Creator and living a life of purpose. Period. All of those things above may be a part of your purpose, but there's more to it. What is your calling? What are your gifts and talents? What is it that makes your soul sing? Don't buy the lies. Passionately pursue your purpose while intimately connecting to the God of the universe. Yes! Live life on purpose and joy will abound!

Superwoman ...a badge of honor or label of bondage?

Let's face it; we all desire to feel important, to be affirmed, to excel at what we put our hands and mind to. The expectations of others or being placed on a pedestal may have earned you the title "Superwoman" and you may wear it proudly. What cost do you pay for that title, for that role? Do you have to always be "on", never allowed to have a bad moment? Do you have to present as if you always have it all together? Is it affecting your ability to get restful sleep? Is it wreaking your mind with anxiety, taking a toll on your body with unexplained aches and pains or weight gain/loss? If you've experienced folks not coming through for you when you needed them (including mama or daddy) or you're praised and admired for being a superwoman, the last thing you want to do is hang up that cape. But, just look at what it's costing you. Peace, joy, health, happiness...You may say, "I'm good. I'm not experiencing any of that." That's great! Wear your cape proudly. If that's not the case, it's time to break through the bondage of that cape. Do you have a hard time extending grace to yourself? Do you find yourself handling more and more of other peoples' stuff? Do you overcommit yourself? Today's a good day to learn to extend grace to yourself, to give folks their stuff back and to say "No" to others more, so that you can emphatically say "Yes" to yourself.

Until your relationship with self is what it should be, your relationships with others will never be what they could be.

Do you love yourself? Do you like yourself? These may seem like strange questions, but every aspect of your life and how you relate to others is directly related to the answer to these questions. If you received (and internalized) the message that you weren't likable or lovable as a little person, the grown woman that you are today has to reckon with that, has to heal from it and has to reject those destructive messages. When you get to the place where you can say (and mean it) that I love myself, I like myself, daggonit I am in love with myself and I'm pretty amazing, that's when you will treat yourself accordingly. You will walk different. You will talk different. You will respect yourself and accept nothing less from anyone else. You will operate in love from a place of want, not a place of need or desperation. You will covet time with self and protect it. You will prioritize your spiritual, mental, emotional and physical well-being. So again I ask you, do you love yourself? Do you like yourself?

Freedom comes through self acceptance. You are fearfully and wonderfully made (Ps. 139:14). Yes, weaknesses, flaws and all!

I have flaws! Ok, I said it. I'm not perfect. I march to the beat of my own drum and I'm ok with that; today. There was a time when I was less secure with myself and not so accepting of the things about me that set me apart. From body features, to the way I think, to my personality, I saw flaws and weaknesses. The more that I got into my word, and began to see myself through God's eyes; the more that I came to appreciate the parts of myself that were once unacceptable. God put special care into making me. To reject myself is to reject His handiwork. I refuse to do that today. He also put special care into making you. Even if no one else can appreciate you in your entirety, you can. My personality allows me to easily connect to others. That's a gift. You have gifts too. You are beautiful. You have so much to offer the world just as you are. Even if no one took the initiative to let you know how amazing you are, that doesn't make you any less amazing. What are you struggling to accept about yourself? What insecurities are you carrying? Are there voices of condemnation and criticism that you need to silence? Learn to appreciate what is uniquely yours. Embrace all of you.

Rather than incessantly focusing energy and effort on what you don't want; set your sights on what you do want and give it all you've got!

What you focus on grows. It's true. Not only does it grow, but if you're focusing on what you don't want eventually it'll begin to consume energy that could be put into what you DO want. If you're focused on the bad relationship, you'll get more of that. If you're focused on the problems around you, more of that will come your way. If you're focused on the parts of yourself that you wish were different, you'll miss out on the opportunity to appreciate the other parts of yourself. Energy and time are not limitless commodities so it's best to focus them on what you want. I want great health, wonderful relationships, financial security, peace...all the good stuff. That's where my focus goes? What do you want? When would you like to have it by? What is already in your possession to get you those things? Go for it!

Making peace with your past ushers in healing that evades denial.

There are some pretty messed up things in my past. Some of these things I contributed to and some of them were someone else's doing. Heck, some stuff can't be attributed to anyone. It just is or was. Making peace with your past means you've looked at your past, accepted it for what it was, and moved forward into your future. Making peace means you're not stuck there or controlled by it. You may still have some of the scars, but they aren't your identity. Making peace isn't about forgetting or denial. It's acknowledging the reality of what was, while leaving room for the limitless possibilities of what can be. What's in your past? Failed relationships? Abuse? Addictions? Betrayal? Abandonment? Violations? Do these things take you to a place of shame, anger, resentment, depression...? Your past isn't really your past if it's here, today, controlling your emotions. Sure, you can experience a memory and find yourself momentarily in a dark place, but when the dark place is home and it's fully furnished, it's time to do whatever's necessary to make peace in a healthy way. There are many ways of making peace. The Christian in me points you to your prayer room. The therapist in me points you to the therapy room. The writer in me points you to your journal. Whatever avenue you take, I pray that healing and wholeness are the end results.

When you start showing up for others more than you show up for yourself, it's time to re-evaluate, rededicate, and reprioritize.

There is something beautiful about knowing that you know that you know that you have your own back. As women the message received tends to be, sacrifice, be there for others, and put your needs on the back burner. Worse more, we're told that we're selfish or inconsiderate when we prioritize our own needs and wants. These internalized messages are sending many a woman to an early grave. You can't give what you don't have, yet many of us are drawing from an empty well and too guilt stricken to tap into full flowing wells. Don't mistreat and neglect yourself. If you can't count on any one else to show up on your behalf, you owe it to yourself to show up for you. Where's the honor in ignoring your own plea for help, for respite? Make a list of the people who can count on you no matter what? Is your name on that list? If not, what message have you heard that says that it's not ok to place yourself as a priority? Is there a certain voice that you hear? What's the message that you can tell yourself to drive it home that it's ok to come through for yourself more than you come through for others? Repeat this message to yourself daily and with conviction. Yes! You deserve the best of you.

When you least feel like working out, is often when you most need it. Yes! Release those endorphins, baby!!!

Let's face it! You're either the type of person
who enjoys working out or you're not. Well, I
guess that's not really true because I have a love-
hate relationship with working out (don't you
hate when you debunk your own thoughts.)
Once I get started, I'm in love, but it's not my
favorite thing to do by far. I've read about how
exercise impacts mood and the mind. What I
experienced firsthand is far more impressive
than the textbook explanation of biology and
anatomy. The natural high is what I'm speaking
of. The one that gives you some get up and go,
some motivation to move ahead, to accomplish
all that lies before you. For me, exercise isn't
just about trying to counter what aging is so
excited to deliver at my feet. It's bigger than
that. It's about a quality of life that makes me
want to have many more tomorrows. Have you
ever felt down and not wanted to do
much? That's a good time to work out, take a
brisk walk. Ever find yourself mad or
frustrated? Of course you have! Release some of
those emotions through exercise to clear your
mind to really address what's going on. Give
your body and mind a healthy dose of what they
need, movement, and exercise. How often do
you exercise? Do you work best solo or with
others? Do you need accountability? Is the
physical and mental rewards enough or do you
need additional incentives to exercise
consistently?

It's not all about you, but sometimes it's **ALL** *about you.*

It's easy to think that the next person's unkind words or snappy attitude is about you. After all, they're sending off a vibe of "Get out of my space" or "You're totally annoying me right now." Believe it or not, the person in front of you may have issues that have nothing to do with you. You just happen to be the closest person to them at the moment or a perceived easy target. They may have just received the worst news imaginable, they may have fallen out with their significant other last night or they may just naturally have the nastiest attitude known to wo(man). It's not about you! Then again, sometimes it's all about you. Your actions or words may bring you face to face with someone who isn't having it. As the old saying goes, you may have met your match. It can be hard to accept this because we often don't see ourselves as being this far gone, or we see ourselves as justified and totally within our rights. The truth can hurt and sting and burn and it has a way of showing up on your doorstep and daring you to deny it. Do you tend to take things personally or step back to get a broader view of the situation? Do you treat others as you'd like to be treated or demand respect regardless of your treatment of others? Do you find it easy to apologize and make amends or is your attitude, "Get over it!" Truly, it's not always about you, but some days it's all about you.

Morning routine: exercise, praise/worship, devotional…

The way that you start your day can mean the difference between feeling more grounded, focused and at peace or ushering in a day full of chaos and confusion and feeling that you're always two steps behind and trying to catch up. You may start each day franticly looking for your misplaced keys and purse or you may start it calmly with everything in its place. Some people have a difficult time imagining a life that's not in disarray, and if that's what turns you on, let it be, but if you want to have a different experience, you may want to try something different. A morning routine in which time with God is the focus works for me. It seems as if I have more time in the day, even if that's not the case. Stress and anxiety decrease, and a sense of balance is present throughout the day. I can tell when I've neglected my routine for a number of days. Things don't seem to go as smoothly and I feel like the dog being wagged by the tail. Life just doesn't feel right. Of course I deviate from my routine from time to time and allow room for spontaneity, but I've found what works for me. What does your morning routine consist of? Does it rejuvenate you for the day or leave you feeling like climbing back in bed by noon? Does your routine leave your entire household in a sour mood or do you set a mellow or upbeat tone for everyone? Do you need to wake up a little earlier to allow for a more peaceful routine or maybe even go to bed a little earlier?

Some of us are carrying baggage that isn't ours, while wearing garments that we've outgrown.

Mama and daddy gave us some things, some good, some bad. Our upbringing and environment gave us some things. What will we do with what we've been given? I surmise that we should hold on to those things that serve us well and cast away those things that do us no good. From prejudices to preferences, we are allowed to decide if we want to challenge them by looking at them deeper or embrace them wholeheartedly. Voices of people long gone may be orchestrating the course of your life in ways that even they never intended. Rumors and hearsay may have you feeling some kind of way based on someone else's experiences. Closing a door based on that is limiting your possibilities. That doesn't have to be the case. On the other hand, you've got your own experiences and thoughts to contend with. You've put on attitudes and have formed beliefs that fit well back then, however, today, they may no longer fit. Have a willingness to re-evaluate and recalibrate and shed those old garments. Keep your eyes open for the garbage that you're carrying that's not yours. Bitterness, resentment, fears, suspicions...If you're anything like me, you've got enough of your own.

Surround yourself with others who: celebrate your success enthusiastically, aren't afraid to call you on your mess, and lend an ear and a shoulder when you need it.

My mother once told me that I was a loner. She was speaking in the sense that as a child, I would be fine solo. I didn't have a lot of friends or need to fit in with the crowd. I was perfectly ok being by myself in my own world. I never really saw myself as a loner, but hey if mama saw me that way, that may have been the case. Today, I intentionally surround myself with "my" people. By this, I mean, people who have my back. People who want the best for me. My people don't have to look anything like me, but they do have to look out for my best interest and let me know when I'm slipping or tripping. Who's in your circle? Is it Negative Nancy or No Nonsense Nikara? Is it Messy Molly or Mellow Myles? Do those in your circle throw shade when you're doing your thing or throw a celebration in honor of you? There are plenty of people in the world who will not be in your corner or cheering you on. That's fine, but they don't belong in your circle. Who's in your circle? What role does each person play? Is there a need that you have from your circle that is not currently filled (encouragement, support, accountability…)? Are you open to expanding or eliminating from your circle?

Prioritizing taking care of self sometimes leaves others wondering where they fit in. That's ok. Continue setting the example and eventually they may also realize that they have the same privilege and obligation.

I was groomed early in life to take care of myself. This later turned into me taking care of others. It started slowly with small tasks then grew into bigger projects that weren't mine and a little of everything in between. I presented as a fully capable person wanting to be of help. I seemed happy doing it and I made it look easy. I was teaching people how to treat me and didn't even realize it. As my desire to focus more on myself and my own life increased, I would attempt to give people their stuff back or to not even accept it from the beginning. Here came the push back. It wasn't ugly push back, but it was push back all the same. It can be difficult because these are people that you love, who also love you. Guilt creeps in and a sense of obligation follows. "Am I being selfish?" "Isn't it better to give than receive?" "Aren't I blessed to be a blessing?" Questions poured in from all sides and made me second guess my decision to set boundaries and put myself at the top of my priority list. I had to push through and do it anyway! Do you find yourself putting your needs at the end of your 'To Do' list? Does guilt or shame show up when you attempt to prioritize taking care of self? Do you need to give anyone their stuff back? This can be very difficult, but the more you take on that's not yours, the less room you have for what IS yours. You are the teacher. Each day you're handing out lessons on how others can treat you. Teach well!

Wisdom says, "Everything that comes to your mind isn't meant to be spoken out of your mouth."

How many thoughts go through the human mind in the span of an hour? Hundreds? Thousands? The "experts" say thousands so let's go with that. With that many thoughts, it's safe to say that it's not even possible to speak each thought. How do you decide which thoughts are "share worthy?" Is it the thoughts that align with what you're passionate about? Is it the thoughts that will rile others up or get under their skin? Is it the thoughts that keep peace and don't ruffle any feathers? Take a minute before speaking and ask yourself, what purpose will what I'm about to speak fulfill. If you're good with the answer, speak it. If not, let that thought remain a thought and keep it to yourself. Once the words leave your lips you can't take them back. Be intentional in what you speak, not careless. Be purposefully passionate, not petty.

God's going to do His part, but will you commit to intentionally showing up for yourself today (through your thoughts, words and actions)?

Intentional: done on purpose, deliberate. Showing up for yourself shouldn't just take place by happenstance. It should be your drive, your goal, your mission. And this should be the case every day. Not once in a while. Daily! There isn't just one area that this should happen in either. It should take place in all areas of your life, from your choices in what you eat to your choices in who you allow in your space. You should be intentional about what you watch and read as well as the words you speak over yourself. Too often people make bad decisions that render negative consequences and are shocked at the outcome. It rains on the just and the unjust (Matt. 5:45), so negative outcomes aren't always a result of any wrongdoing or decision that someone has made, but in many cases it is. Failing to act at all is the culprit at times as well. It's like we're paralyzed and unable to make a decision. Life goes on and a decision is made for us which can be much worse than what would have come from our own deliberate action. How deliberate are you in showing up for yourself (spiritually, emotionally, physically, relationally...)? What is one thing that you can do with intention in each area of your life to show up for yourself like never before?

Worry has stolen many a moment, from many a day, from many a souls, in many a day.

As I sit here writing, I have knots in my stomach. I have a 6 am flight leaving for Florida en route to the Bahamas and I'm wondering is my scheduled transportation going to show up at 3:30 am. After all, it is 0 degrees out with the temperature continuing to drop. Surely, no one's trying to come out in the wee hours of the morning to get little ol' me (and my hubby). Worry is a thief. It takes the good in each moment and evaporates it until there's nothing left. Right now I should be ecstatic about escaping this frigid cold and walking on a warm beach, but no, I'm worrying about something that's really a nonissue (we have cars and can drive ourselves). Worry is a thief and a liar. It tells us that we have no options or the only ones we have are bleak. LIES!!! Does worry get the best of you at times? Does your faith help you in times of worry? What do you need to tell yourself or envision to change your perspective and put the lying thief in its place? Right now, I'm thinking warm beach, sand, slushy mixed concoctions...

Grace says that I don't have to get it all right (and neither do you).

What is grace to you? Is it what you say before a meal? Is it elegance or poise? Grace is all of those things, but it's also the thing that literally changed my life, once I fully understood it. Grace allows me to be human. It allows me to fail, mess up, and still be whole. Grace goes to war with the superwoman in me and usually wins. It tells her to sit down and chill out. It tells her that she doesn't have to be perfect or strive to be anything that she is not. Grace is truly my bestie. Her favorite phrase is, "It's ok." I guess she's not much for words, but the way that I feel in her presence is free, loved, accepted, good enough... My goal is to introduce Grace to each person I meet. We have enough people who judge and condemn. Just one, "It's ok" may give enough hope to sustain life one more day. Everyone needs a Grace in their life. Grace was introduced to me by Jesus Christ. Like I said, my life has never been the same. Is Grace a constant companion or is condemnation? How might your life look differently if Grace visited you more often?

Ever find your plate full of others' responsibilities? Give one (or several) thing(s) back today to make room for what's needed to fulfill your purpose.

I gave a brief overview of the superwoman syndrome at a networking meeting and later was asked to facilitate a workshop on the same topic. One of the participants from the networking mixer approached me before I facilitated the workshop and stated that she was using the piece that I had shared about giving people their stuff back and it was making a big difference in her life. Here's the short and sweet version. We go through life picking up and being given other people's stuff. After a while we have so much stuff that isn't ours, we can't give the due attention to what is ours. We may become resentful or feel taken for granted, but we still hold on to it for various reasons, "He's not capable of handling his business." "It's no big deal. I can do it." "I can't tell her 'No'. That would mess up our relationship." Whatever the story you tell yourself, realize that enabling someone to do for themselves is good, enabling someone to shirk their responsibilities is not good. When you say "Yes" to their stuff, what stuff of your own are you saying "No" to? Maybe you feel that other people's stuff is your responsibility or there's no way around it. Look for ways to have balance, reach out for help if needed, and give back what you can.

Feeling ignored by others can be annoying, but how often do you fail to listen to yourself and give yourself what you need?

Have you ever been in a conversation and realize that the person you're talking to has checked out? They may still be there physically, but they're not taking in your words. Or maybe you've called across the room to get someone's attention and they continue doing what they're doing and don't acknowledge you? If you've never experienced this, let me just say, it doesn't feel good. Not at all. It may anger you or make you feel really small and insignificant. Well, we tend to ignore ourselves at times also. You've got an unexplainable pain and you don't slow down long enough to check in to see what it may be. You're upset about a situation, but you make yourself move past it before checking in and comforting yourself. You have a gut feeling about a situation, but you subdue your gut rather than checking in to see what you need in the situation. It can be as simple as needing a nap or needing a snack. Your body, mind and spirit are always reaching out. You decide whether you'll push the ignore button or accept. Do you check in with yourself regularly to see where you're at and what you need? If so, what have these check-ins revealed? How have you responded? If not, how might your relationship with self look different if you made a habit of checking in with self and giving yourself what you need.

It's fascinating how the mind and body protest the overwhelming demands that we place on them.

The mind and body are marvelous wonders. Two people can go through the same experience, relatively speaking, and one emerge with greater resilience and one emerge broken and bankrupt. One person can come through the horrors of cancer and go into remission while another succumbs to it. Our minds and bodies go through a lot in the course of a day, a week, and a lifetime. Sometimes we put more on them than they can bear and then we curse God saying, "You said you'd never give me more than I could bear." If he hasn't spoken to you about that, let me help you out. 1. He won't give you more than you can bear With Him and 2. Some of that stuff, He didn't give you and never wanted you to have. The mind and body have ways of telling us that we need to slow down, regroup and reprioritize. That doesn't mean that every illness or complication in life is due to an issue on your part, but it would behoove you to treat your mind and body with care. Don't run them in the ground and then wonder why they can't go any further. PROTEST! What does your physical and mental wellness routine look like? How do you know that you need to slow down? Don't overwhelm your great gifts. Treat them with loving kindness and care.

One of the most beautiful gifts that you can give yourself is learning to love your own company.

When you don't enjoy your own company you're more likely to settle for the company of those who don't deserve your presence. I hear people refer to being bored when alone. How is this so? You have the ability to talk/listen to, entertain, and create an atmosphere uniquely suited to you. Your thoughts can be unapologetically expressed and acknowledged. You can be as chill or as hype as you desire. Yes! What a gift! Do you enjoy time alone? If not, what makes time alone less enjoyable than time with others? Take some time to get to know yourself. You're not the same person that you were 5 years ago, 10 years ago or even last week. With each new experience comes a new you. As you cast away the judgments, likes/dislikes and preferences of others, what you enjoy will surface. Sometimes while in the company of others, a desire to please others takes precedence. There's a time and a place for yielding to others and there's a time to give yourself the gift of careful consideration and genuine intrigue and curiosity. Yes! You are worth taking the time to get to know yourself and acknowledge what is discovered.

Some issues are 'Dad' sized. Use wisdom. There's no need to suffer alone.

My earthly father is amazing. Sure he has his issues, as we all do, but I know without a shadow of a doubt that he'd drop whatever he was doing to come to my aid in a heartbeat. Your earthly father may be amazing as well or he may have been absent, a jerk or somewhere in between. However, as awesome as my earthly father is, there are many issues that I would never bring to him. They are 'Dad' sized and require the help of my Heavenly Father. You too have issues that require the help of your Heavenly Father. Do you go to your Daddy when in need or find yourself trying to figure it out on your own? Do you call on sources that can't really provide the solution you need or reach out through prayer with great expectations of answers, breakthroughs, deliverance, healing...? He may not answer the way that you would like or when you would like, but He's got your back. Through the good, the bad, the best and worst, He has a listening ear, a lap and a shoulder. Let Him be the caring Father that only He can be.

You are ENOUGH... smart enough, beautiful enough, creative enough...

In a world that is constantly telling us all the things that we need to change to measure up, to be successful, to be ENOUGH...it's easy to get caught up in the deception. You may have been told by your own mother, your own father what you need to do to get up to par. Media may hold up images of beauty that look nothing like you and you find yourself comparing, analyzing and trying to conform to what you see. From the marks on the report card that told you your ranking, to the titles, to the digits on the scale, there's always more to strive towards, one more step that needs to be taken to prove that you're enough. NONSENSE! You are enough TODAY with all of your flaws and idiosyncrasies. Yes, you are...fearfully and wonderfully made (Ps. 139:14). Do you find yourself struggling to believe that you are enough? Is there a dominant voice that you hear telling you all the ways that you need to change? If so, how can you counter those beliefs, those words, with the truth? I suggest you begin by digging into your word to see what God has to say about you.

*Who would have
thought that 45
could feel so
amazing! Blessed
beyond measure
by the BEST!!!*

Each year that passes gives me a new appreciation for life. We've all heard the phrase, "tomorrow's not promised to anyone." That's true and gratitude for each new day is a good thing; however, we also have to wrestle with our own mortality, ageism, and the highs and lows of "maturing." What do you appreciate most about your current age? Is there anything that you're having a difficult time coming to terms with related to your age? Sometimes you just need to bring what's on the inside out in order to heal, to learn to grow. Talk to your girlfriends. Grab the ear of an advisor or mentor that may have traveled the same road. Ahhh...there's nothing like bringing light to your situations.

Talks with my Father, a good book, aromatherapy, hot stone massages, quality time with my Honey…a few of the things that make my soul sing!

What makes your soul sing? What makes your eyes widen and makes you take a deep breath? What gives you butterflies in your stomach (the good kind) and makes you giddy like a little girl. Well girl, incorporate more of that into your life. Be a little adventurous. Try new things to get a better idea of what you like and don't like. If you're saying, "Girl, I know full well what I like", well ok, do more of that. Your singing soul reverberates and sends great positive energy out to the world. We need your soul to sing. Yes, you need your soul to sing. A songless soul is the breeding ground for bitterness and resentment. What are 5 things that make your soul sing? How often do you engage in these things? What are 2 things that you can do less of (because they really don't make your soul sing at all) in order to have more time for what does make your soul sing?

Regardless of what's going on in the world around you, your inner world can be at peace.

Turn on the news for 5 minutes and you'll be inundated with bad news, sad news, death and destruction. Simply by answering your phone the problems of the person on the other end can quickly become yours. One moment everything can seem fine and the next all hell can be breaking loose. Do I have a witness? It's important to be able to maintain your peaceful state when the world around you seems as if it's falling apart. If not, you may feel like you're on a yoyo, up one minute and down the next. Peace is a gift from God. It's your birthright. When anxiety begins to creep in and your stomach is in knots, thank God for His peace that surpasses all understanding (Phil. 4:7). Give Him what's His, all the mess that you can't control and rest assured that He'll take care of it. That doesn't excuse you from doing what is in your control, but peace comes in knowing that you don't have to have it all figured out. Write down the things that are robbing you of peace today? Put an "M" (for mine) next to those things that are in your control to change. Put a "G" (for God) next to those things that are outside of your control. Give God what's His and do what you need to do to handle the rest.

When we remove our masks, the vulnerability can be scary; however, true intimacy (with ourselves and others) requires nakedness!

A mask is worn to hide the true identity of a person. Sometimes even with the mask on, there are enough facial features still exposed that others have a pretty good idea of who's behind the mask. Other times that's not the case. We sometimes spend years trying to create the perfect mask that will cover up those parts of us that we don't want others to see. Sometimes we wear our masks so long that we forget who we are or even fool ourselves into thinking that the mask is our true identity. Healing is impossible behind the mask and so is genuine connection with others. "Will I be accepted if I expose my truth?" "Will my vulnerabilities be exploited?" "Who am I really without the facade of my mask?" You may find yourself asking these questions and others. First, it's most important that you acknowledge the truth of who you are with yourself. This truth is made up of where you come from, your experiences, and the messages that have helped to form you into who you are today. Equally as important to acknowledge is what drives and motivates you to wake up in the morning and do all the things that you do. Is it a sense of purpose and passion or a sense of obligation, guilt or shame?

A heart of gratitude opens up a whole new world.

Thank you! Thank you! Thank you! There's something about gratitude, thankfulness that makes my heart happy. I've been through my fair share of hard times, but being grateful even in the midst of difficulties seems to make the bad more bearable and the good that is to come, arrive more quickly. Gratefulness leaves room for countless possibilities. It puts a crack in the dismal, making way for a ray of light. How does it feel to you when someone extends gratitude your way? It may take you aback because many feel that it's not necessary to do, but probably feels really good when it happens. You probably want to extend yourself more for this person because they are genuinely grateful. I can imagine the same is true for God. When one of His children is genuinely grateful He probably desires to rain down more blessings and more blessings (this is my take on it, so no need to go super theological on me). What is something that you have been struggling with lately? What would it look like for you to have a grateful heart even in the midst of your struggles? Write 3-5 things that you're grateful for at the close of each day. Expect a whole new world to open up.

Expect great things! Don't get caught up in negativity or mediocrity!

Your thoughts create your reality. If you
expect that things will never go your way,
there is a great chance that they won't. If you
expect favor, abundance and blessings, watch
out because here they come. Of course you
have to also work for your greater good, but
your positive mindset is the breeding ground
for an overflow of good. Negativity, on the
other hand, is like the flu. Hang around it long
enough and you'll find yourself with the chills
(complaining), a fever (irritable), diarrhea
(gossiping), and body aches (discontent).
Yuck, is right! It can be so insidious and sneak
up on you so quickly that you have no idea
that it's now a part of you or even where you
picked it up. Mediocrity is also one of those
mindset things. You're uniquely gifted for
something, so don't get caught up in the ho-
hum of each day and not pursue what it is that
only you can do, in the spectacular way that
you can do it. Are you expecting greatness in
your life? Do you believe all of the resources
you need are at your disposal? Are there
people you need to give some space to, so that
you can shake off the negativity bug? Are you
pushing forth in your purpose, pushing pause
or sending out invitations to your pity party?

If you carried bitterness and resentment from last year into this year or you're still carrying it from 5/10 years ago, commit to dealing with it. Don't let bitterness or resentment rob you of your peace.

I can see some heads shaking right now. "I'm not bitter! I'm better!" "I don't have a problem. It's them." "He/she deserves this wrath. Look what they did to me." Hey, if you can hold that stance and be at peace, more power to you. But, it's not possible to be at peace while carrying a duffle bag or pulling a dump truck of bitterness and resentment. Sorry, not possible. Deal with whatever is making you feel some kind of way and move forward. That doesn't mean you won't have to ever deal with those folks who have hurt you ever again. It also doesn't mean that you should cut every person off who has ever wronged you. It's much more complex than that. As a therapist, I see the fruit of unresolved pain. It eats away at the soul like cancer and leaves you emaciated, clinging on for life. The quality of life is not what it could or should be. Make a list of the people who have harmed you in one way or another. Find a healthy way of expressing the pain, the anger, the resentment. Grieve what you've loss through this person's/systems actions, words, etc...and move forward with your life. (I would highly suggest working through this process with a qualified professional. Opening doors to things that you're unable to properly address can be very dangerous.)

Shift your mindset and life so that you can emphatically proclaim TGIM, TGIW…!

Do you live for the weekend? Is Monday through Thursday painstakingly hard to face? Change your mental space and life so that you can look forward to each new day. You may be asking, "How do I do that when I have to go to a job that I don't like, to work with folks that I don't like?" Or you may feel that your routine is so mundane, day in and day out, with endless responsibilities and the weekend offers your only respite or turn up time. You may not be able to make the shift right away, but you can begin to gradually make changes to your routine and add elements into each day that you can look forward to. This may come in the form of a fun exercise class, music interludes, or even quality time catching up with your girl friends or guy friends. You may be more emboldened and ready to take a leap of faith to get from a place that you don't like, to one with the possibility to feed your soul. Do it! Of course you'll have to put the work in, but 20, 30, 40 years of misery should never be an option. Do you live for the weekend? If so, are you ok with that or do you want more? What would need to take place in order for you to find fulfillment in the other days of the week? What changes do you need to make in your thinking in order to see your Monday through Thursday life differently?

What is success without peace, without joy?

How do you spell success, "m o n e y?" Or maybe you spell it, "p o w e r." Some spell it, "a c c o m p l i s h m e n t s" or "f a m e." Regardless of what denotes success to you, without peace and joy, what do you have? It hurts my heart to see a person who outwardly has all the catchings of success who is torn up on the inside, emotionally bankrupt. Chances are they're self medicating just to get from day to day. Whether this self medicating comes in the form of sex, drugs, gambling, food or shopping, that's irrelevant. Life without peace and joy leaves a void that no amount of success can fill. If this wasn't the case there wouldn't be so many people, seemingly, with everything that you could ever imagine who are self destructing. If you stripped away all of your remnants of success, what would remain? What have you buried that continues to rear its ugly head? Who sold you a lie about what does/doesn't constitute success? Set out on a journey to gain greater peace and joy today.

Create the life you want!

I recall sitting in my cubicle several years ago, a little miserable, having a pity party of sorts. I was not happy with where I was in life and felt helpless to change my situation. I remember distinctly hearing God tell me, "Create the life you want." I don't hear God in that way often, so let's just say He got my attention. From that day forward I've been on a mission. This mission required me to get really clear about my purpose and my passion in life. It required me to make some hard decisions and big sacrifices. It required me to stop making excuses and start being more accountable. Man! I see why it took a wake-up call from my Father before I sprung into action because there was nothing easy about the process from A to M (I'm still in the process). There are so many things that I want to do for others and experience for myself and I'm the only one standing in my way. My happiness rests on no one else's shoulders and neither does my anguish or discontent. The same goes for you. You're a co-creator with the Most High. Don't settle for less. In what areas of your life are you throwing a pity party? Is it your career, your relationships, your finances...? Create the life you want!

"I love you!"
"You're so
beautiful!" "You're
amazing!" Why
wait to be bathed in
others' affirming
words when you
can shower yourself
daily?

People can be so fickle. Today they love you, tomorrow they don't. Today you're the most beautiful person in their eyes; tomorrow they find 1000 flaws with your looks. Today you earn their accolades, tomorrow they mean nothing. Just face it; if you leave it to others to inflate you and tell you your worth, you risk being deflated at any given moment. Affirm yourself! Yes, I said it! Affirm yourself. It's not about arrogance or ego. It's all about giving yourself a healthy dose of self love. No one can take that from you. Look in the mirror and tell yourself how beautiful you are, after all, you're made in God's image and after His likeness (Gen. 1:26). If He's all that and a bag of chips, so are you. If He's amazingly awesome, so are you. Do you struggle with affirming yourself? Do you see your strengths and acknowledge them? Do you see your beauty, inside and out, and acknowledge it? Do you walk with your head held high knowing that you're a special unique individual, whether you're all dolled up or in sweats and a ball cap? Straighten your crown Queen and take your rightful place.

Shhhh! Take a minute to sit in silence. Chaos, drama and chatter want to become your norm. Don't let them!

There is nothing like silence, being left
alone with your own thoughts, void of the
clamor of noise, hustle and bustle. There are
so many forces always vying for our
attention, persistently demanding space in
our minds. It can be so draining. It can also
be attractive, alluring. Who's doing what and
what's popping off where can be a
welcomed distraction to what's going on in
your own world. Sitting with your own
thoughts can be unbearable to some. Painful
memories may await you and guilt and
shame may want their due time. Do you
struggle with silence? Are intrusive thoughts
an issue for you? If that's the case, get help
processing what you aren't able to work
through by yourself and move on. Take a
minute to meditate. Practice mindfulness to
ground yourself in the present. Reclaim your
thoughts, your solitude.

Today is as good a day as any to face the paralyzing fears, expel the unrealistic expectations, and breakdown the limiting beliefs that stand between you and your amazing tomorrow.

Fear has kept me from achieving many things in the past. For some it may be hard to believe because outwardly I can appear to be fearless, but inwardly I deal with paralyzing fear sometimes. This is the type of fear that stops me dead in my tracks and lets life make decisions for me because I refuse to do so myself. This is the fear that whispers to me that I can't do it, it won't work out, and no one will support me. This fear brings about limiting beliefs that are ingrained. You too may know this fear. I've adapted a new mindset in some ways that helps me to combat this fear. I think to myself, "And?" In other words, if my worst fear is true, so what? I will do what I can do and leave the rest to someone else. This may be man, but often times it's God. He doesn't expect me to do more than I can and He has equipped me for great works. Fear tries to render me an amnesiac. The truth is the last thing it wants me to recall. In what ways does fear invade your space? What truths does fear want you to forget? Has fear set up limiting (false) beliefs within you? Dismantle the fear, brick by brick. Don't succumb to it. You're unstoppable!

I pray that you saved a little for yourself…a little grace, a little peace a little time, a little understanding, a little laughter…

If you're like me, you know all too well the feeling of giving the best piece of meat to someone else, giving the best seat, giving the best... No doubt, it's ok to give, but don't forget to save some for yourself. The meat or the seat aren't really what I'm speaking of or maybe they are. My question is, are you giving away all of your best to others and not keeping any of the good for yourself? Are you able to accept others' human frailties, but expecting perfection from yourself? Are you always interceding to bring peace to others while internally you're in flux? Do you always have a listening ear, a shoulder for others to cry on and wish you had the same for yourself? You may need to step back for a minute and give yourself room to give yourself what you need and to make room for someone else to pour into you as well. Save some of the good stuff for yourself. Folks are watching to see how they should treat you and the best example of that is how you treat yourself.

What do you need?
More stuff? More
titles? More
"friends?" Nope!
Not hardly! Not
really! Take a minute
and ask yourself
what you really need
and come through
for yourself like
never before!

I recently facilitated a workshop for women who self identified as superwomen. At the end of the workshop each woman had an opportunity to express a need to the group and to receive encouragement and support in return. I could see the wheels turning in these women's heads as they thought about what it was that they were in need of. When it pertains to material things it's easy to identify the need, however, when it comes time to look at our own emotional, spiritual, and relational needs, it's far more difficult. When's the last time you had a heart to heart with yourself and asked yourself what it is that you need? Is there a yearning to be comforted, to be understood, to be accepted? Well, you can give those things to yourself. If you don't show up for yourself in the most crucial times, why should you expect someone else to? What do you need? Listen to your heart. Listen to your mind. Now, give it!!!

"Who signed me up for all this?" *Be careful of overcommitting yourself. What's truly important will suffer in the end.*

Years ago my aunt told me the story of a little boy; we'll call him Little Billy, in her 1st grade class. She said after lunch Little Billy was nowhere to be found. After checking all around inside the school Little Billy was found sitting on the steps outside of the school. She approached Little Billy and asked him where he was going. She told him that there was still so much to do, there was reading and math and writing to do. She said Little Billy looked up at her and asked, "Who signed me up for all this s**t?" Unlike Little Billy who was struggling with the adjustment from a half day and play in kindergarten, you may be struggling because you're constantly piling your plate with commitments on top of commitments. You're trying to juggle it all and you're either late to this or missing that all together. You keep signing yourself up for things that have nothing to do with your purpose; in fact, you can't even fully fulfill your purpose because of all the extra. Boss Lady, you need a break! A break from yourself. You need to fire yourself as your scheduler and put a new you in that role! One that refuses to take on more and more to your own detriment. Are you afraid to say, "No?" Do you think you have to fulfill every need that's brought before you? Does it feel selfish to tend to what's yours and let others tend to what's theirs? Whatever the issue may be, get to the bottom of it and free yourself. Your purpose needs you!

God clearly told me not long ago, "You have all you need."

Have you ever wanted to step out and do something only to find that you need XY and Z in order to make it happen? Kind of like waiting for the perfect moment that will never happen. I was in that place, not long ago actually, and God clearly spoke to me and said, "You have all you need." Less than a handful of times I've heard God speak to me in that way, so once again, I took heed. I don't think He was frustrated with me, but I could see Him shaking His head like, "Really? Not this again." I couldn't even argue because it was undeniably true. Fear was bigger, in this instance, than faith. It's sad to say, but true. You may be wondering, where faith comes in if I have all that I need. All that I need can't be seen by the naked eye, can't be touched. All that I need is already in me. Faith allows me to access it. As a child of the Living God, I have His spirit. What more do I need? The degrees, connections, and experience are great, but they pale to the power within me. If the spirit of the Living God lives in you, you have all that you need. What are you going to do with it?

From time to time submerge yourself into the world of children: play, laughter, lightness, and just being tend to come so much more easily.

I love children. I love my grandbabies. I love my nephews and nieces and my little cousins. When children come to our home, I come to their level. We play. We cook. We have talent shows and dance. I'm a big kid myself, but they give me permission to be just a little freer. Their anticipation of the fun to be had is great to witness. And I try not to disappoint by being consumed with my electronic devices or other "adult" stuff. The ways their eyes light up (even the cool ones can't contain their excitement) is worth all the effort. So, why do we lose that part of ourselves? If you haven't, that's great! But why is it so hard to just be? Why is *too* much laughter frowned upon? Why are we told to be serious, to grow up? I'll do the adult thing, but every chance I get I'm "kidding." Do you take breaks from adulting to indulge the kid in you? If not, why not? How often do you laugh? Daily? Rarely? Never? Play, laugh, be light, be free.

Commitment can be scary...even to therapy

As you've move through these pages, there may be a few things that have come to light that you thought were a thing of the past. Traumas and past hurts may have resurfaced. While it is never my intent to bring about pain to anyone, I realize that a festering wound that appears to be healed is still a festering wound. It needs to be uncovered, carefully cleaned and protected during the healing process. So does your heart. So does your mind. The right environment is crucial. An environment that's conducive for healing is paramount. As a therapist, it's my job to create this environment. Unfortunately, many will never walk through those doors for various reasons. They may not want to be stigmatized. They may have been told that therapy is for crazy people. They may feel that their problems don't warrant that type of intervention. As I begin to wrap up these 45 lessons in intentionally loving you, I implore you to open your mind to the possibility of healing through the gift of another's presence, witnessing, attunement… Leery? Stick your toe in. Schedule a consultation. YES! Therapy can be an amazing part of your healing journey.

Father, how sweet it is to be loved by You!

I say that I'm your favorite, when I know that all of Your children are Your favorites. It's hard to believe that You have so many children, yet You are there for me whenever I need You. If it concerns me, it concerns You. Big or small, it doesn't matter. You bathe me in your love daily and for that I'm grateful. A loving father I have here on Earth, but your love is greater, you are my Daddy. The love of all pales to Your love. My prayer is that every person who picks up this book feels your overwhelming love. I pray that You shower each one in Your grace and mercy, that You greet them with special surprises each day. Pour out Your peace that surpasses all understanding, that all will know that You are undeniably the Living God.

Now what?

Applied knowledge is PRICELESS! What will you do with what you've picked up through these 45 lessons in intentionally loving you? If you're a superwoman, you're probably planning to tackle 10 things in the next week. Boss Lady, it's not a sprint! This is about making it through this thing called life whole and intact. I suggest you look at 1-2 goals that you'd like to focus on for the next 60 days. After you've gotten a handle on these, look at 1-2 more goals. The goal is to learn to put yourself on the front burner and not sacrifice your sanity, your health for anyone. Besides, what good are you to your family, your friends, your job, your community…if you're no longer here.

Here's to an abundance of love, peace and joy in your life!

Use the following pages to outline your goals and track your progress. Remember to focus on 1-2 goals at a time. If you find yourself attempting to achieve all of your goals at once, stop for a minute and evaluate why you feel the need to accomplish everything at once. Here are some possible goals:

to give_____ his/her _____back.

to set aside _____ minutes a day to

_____.

to not accept any new projects in the next _____ days/weeks.

to schedule a physical check-up by_____.

to go to bed by _____ each night.

These are some basic examples. In reading the 45 lessons you probably felt a tug on your heart letting you know that there was an area needing your attention. Focus on the areas that are most crucial for your well-being first.

Goal 1:

My goal is:_____

_____

_____

_____

I would like to achieve this goal by:_____

_____

I will know that I have achieved my goal

when:_____

_____

The first thing that I need to do in working

towards this goal is:_____

_____

_____

An obstacle that may make achieving this

goal difficult is:_____

_____

My strengths that can be used to help me

achieve this goal are:_____

_____

_____

Accountability partners for this goal are:

_____

_____

I will celebrate or acknowledge the

achievement of this goal by:_____

_____

_____

Week 1 Progress and/or Setbacks:_____

_____

_____

_____

_____

Week 2 Progress and/or Setbacks:_____

_____

_____

_____

_____

Week 3 Progress and/or Setbacks:_____

_____

_____

_____

_____

Week 4 Progress and/or Setbacks:_____

_____

_____

_____

_____

Week 5 Progress and/or Setbacks:_____

_____

_____

_____

Week 6 Progress and/or Setbacks:_____

_____

_____

_____

_____

Week 7 Progress and/or Setbacks:_____

_____

_____

_____

_____

Week 8 Progress and/or Setbacks:_____

_____

_____

_____

_____

Goal 2:

My goal is:_____

_____

_____

_____

I would like to achieve this goal by:_____

_____

I will know that I have achieved my goal

when:_____

_____

The first thing that I need to do in working

towards this goal is:_____

_____

_____

An obstacle that may make achieving this

goal difficult is:_____

_____

My strengths that can be used to help me

achieve this goal are:_____

_____

_____

Accountability partners for this goal are:

_____

_____

I will celebrate or acknowledge the

achievement of this goal by:_____

_____

_____

Week 1 Progress and/or Setbacks:_____

_____

_____

_____

_____

Week 2 Progress and/or Setbacks:_____

_____

_____

_____

_____

Week 3 Progress and/or Setbacks:_____

_____

_____

_____

_____

Week 4 Progress and/or Setbacks:_____

_____

_____

_____

Week 5 Progress and/or Setbacks:_____

_____

_____

_____

Week 6 Progress and/or Setbacks:_____

_____

_____

_____

_____

Week 7 Progress and/or Setbacks:_____

_____

_____

_____

_____

Week 8 Progress and/or Setbacks:_____

_____

_____

_____

_____

Goal 1:

My goal is:_____

_____

_____

_____

I would like to achieve this goal by:_____

_____

I will know that I have achieved my goal

when:_____

_____

The first thing that I need to do in working

towards this goal is:_____

_____

_____

An obstacle that may make achieving this

goal difficult is:_____

_____

My strengths that can be used to help me

achieve this goal are:_____

_____

_____

Accountability partners for this goal are:

_____

_____

I will celebrate or acknowledge the

achievement of this goal by:_____

_____

_____

Week 1 Progress and/or Setbacks:_____

_____

_____

_____

_____

Week 2 Progress and/or Setbacks:_____

_____

_____

_____

_____

Week 3 Progress and/or Setbacks:_____

_____

_____

_____

_____

Week 4 Progress and/or Setbacks:_____

_____

_____

_____

Week 5 Progress and/or Setbacks:_____

_____

_____

_____

Week 6 Progress and/or Setbacks:_____

_____

_____

_____

_____

Week 7 Progress and/or Setbacks:_____

_____

_____

_____

_____

Week 8 Progress and/or Setbacks:_____

_____

_____

_____

_____

Goal 2:

My goal is:_____

_____

_____

_____

I would like to achieve this goal by:_____

_____

I will know that I have achieved my goal

when:_____

_____

The first thing that I need to do in working

towards this goal is:_____

_____

_____

An obstacle that may make achieving this

goal difficult is:_____

_____

My strengths that can be used to help me

achieve this goal are:_____

_____

_____

Accountability partners for this goal are:

_____

_____

I will celebrate or acknowledge the

achievement of this goal by:_____

_____

_____

Week 1 Progress and/or Setbacks:_____

_____

_____

_____

_____

Week 2 Progress and/or Setbacks:_____

_____

_____

_____

_____

Week 3 Progress and/or Setbacks:_____

_____

_____

_____

_____

Week 4 Progress and/or Setbacks:_____

_____

_____

_____

_____

Week 5 Progress and/or Setbacks:_____

_____

_____

_____

_____

Week 6 Progress and/or Setbacks:_____

_____

_____

_____

_____

Week 7 Progress and/or Setbacks:_____

_____

_____

_____

_____

Week 8 Progress and/or Setbacks:_____

_____

_____

_____

_____

Goal 1:

My goal is:_____

_____

_____

_____

I would like to achieve this goal by:_____

_____

I will know that I have achieved my goal

when:_____

_____

The first thing that I need to do in working

towards this goal is:_____

_____

_____

An obstacle that may make achieving this

goal difficult is:_____

_____

My strengths that can be used to help me

achieve this goal are:_____

_____

_____

Accountability partners for this goal are:

_____

_____

I will celebrate or acknowledge the

achievement of this goal by:_____

_____

_____

Week 1 Progress and/or Setbacks:_____

_____

_____

_____

_____

Week 2 Progress and/or Setbacks:_____

_____

_____

_____

_____

Week 3 Progress and/or Setbacks:_____

_____

_____

_____

_____

Week 4 Progress and/or Setbacks:_____

_____

_____

_____

_____

Week 5 Progress and/or Setbacks:_____

_____

_____

_____

Week 6 Progress and/or Setbacks:_____

_____

_____

_____

_____

Week 7 Progress and/or Setbacks:_____

_____

_____

_____

_____

Week 8 Progress and/or Setbacks:_____

_____

_____

_____

_____

Goal 2:

My goal is:_____

_____

_____

_____

I would like to achieve this goal by:_____

_____

I will know that I have achieved my goal

when:_____

_____

The first thing that I need to do in working

towards this goal is:_____

_____

_____

An obstacle that may make achieving this

goal difficult is:_____

_____

My strengths that can be used to help me

achieve this goal are:_____

_____

_____

Accountability partners for this goal are:

_____

_____

I will celebrate or acknowledge the

achievement of this goal by:_____

_____

_____

Week 1 Progress and/or Setbacks:_____

_____

_____

_____

_____

Week 2 Progress and/or Setbacks:_____

_____

_____

_____

_____

Week 3 Progress and/or Setbacks:_____

_____

_____

_____

Week 4 Progress and/or Setbacks:_____

_____

_____

_____

_____

Week 5 Progress and/or Setbacks:_____

_____

_____

_____

_____

Week 6 Progress and/or Setbacks:_____

_____

_____

_____

_____

Week 7 Progress and/or Setbacks:_____

_____

_____

_____

_____

Week 8 Progress and/or Setbacks:_____

_____

_____

_____

_____

To learn more about Shar'ron's work as a Therapist, Speaker and Author and to purchase her previously released book, Marriage Ain't for Punks, and other products visit her site at ***lovethatrelationship.com***

for couples, for singles, for you

Made in USA - Kendallville, IN
1184051_9780578468709
10.22.2020 1507